W9-BWG-310

MILK

by Gretchen Will Mayo

Reading consultant: Susan Nations, M.Ed., author/literacy coach/consultant

WEEKLY WR READER®
EARLY LEARNING LIBRARY

Please visit our web site at: www.earlyliteracy.cc
For a free color catalog describing Weekly Reader® Early Learning Library's
list of high-quality books, call 1-877-445-5824 (USA) or 1-800-387-3178 (Canada).
Weekly Reader® Early Learning Library's fax: (414) 336-0164.

Library of Congress Cataloging-in-Publication Data

Mayo, Gretchen.
    Milk / by Gretchen Will Mayo.
       p. cm. — (Where does our food come from?)
    Summary: Discusses cow's milk, how it comes from dairy farm animals, and how
it is transformed into various dairy products.
    Includes bibliographical references and index.
    ISBN 0-8368-4067-4 (lib. bdg.)
    ISBN 0-8368-4074-7 (softcover)
    1. Milk—Juvenile literature. 2. Dairying—Juvenile literature. 3. Dairy products—
Juvenile literature. [1. Milk. 2. Dairying. 3. Dairy products.] I. Title.
SF239.5.M39   2004
637'.1—dc22   2003060951

This edition first published in 2004 by
Weekly Reader® Early Learning Library
330 West Olive Street, Suite 100
Milwaukee, WI 53212 USA

Copyright © 2004 by Weekly Reader® Early Learning Library

Editor: JoAnn Early Macken
Art direction, cover and layout design: Tammy Gruenewald
Photo research: Diane Laska-Swanke

Photo credits: Cover, title, pp. 4, 6, 7, 8, 9, 11, 12, 13, 14, 15, 16, 17, 19, 20, 21 © Gregg Andersen;
pp. 10, 18 © Tammy Gruenewald

Printed in the United States of America

1 2 3 4 5 6 7 8 9 08 07 06 05 04

Table of Contents

Three cheers for a snack of cold milk!

Good for Bones and Teeth

Smart kids know that milk is good for them. You can drink milk any time of day. You should drink milk with your meals.

Milk is rich in calcium. It contains protein and vitamins, too. Milk helps make bones and teeth strong. Two to three servings of dairy products a day help keep us healthy.

Can you find milk on the food pyramid?

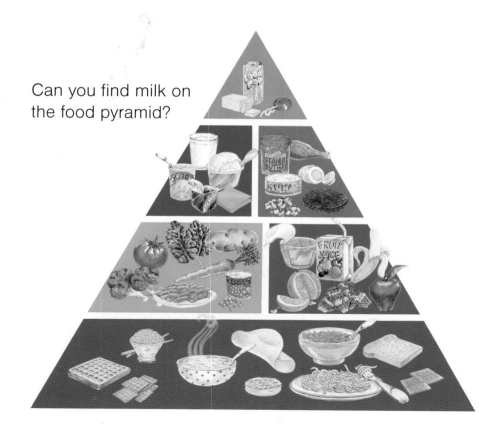

Some people prefer to drink goat's milk.

On a Dairy Farm

Many breeds of cows produce milk. Other animals, such as goats and sheep, also make milk that people can drink.

In the United States, the Holstein is the most popular dairy cow. It can produce more milk than other breeds. It can produce up to 8 gallons (30 liters) a day.

Holstein cows have black and white markings.

Holstein dairy cows graze, or eat grass, slowly.

Dairy cows spend most of their time eating.
During warm months, a dairy cow grazes in a field.
It eats about 50 pounds (23 kilograms) of grass a
day. It drinks about 16 gallons (60 l) of water a day.

During cold months, many cows move into barns.
Farmers give them dried hay, grains, and silage to
eat. Silage is food that is cut while it is still green.
It is held in silos for winter use.

Cows eat silage in a barn.

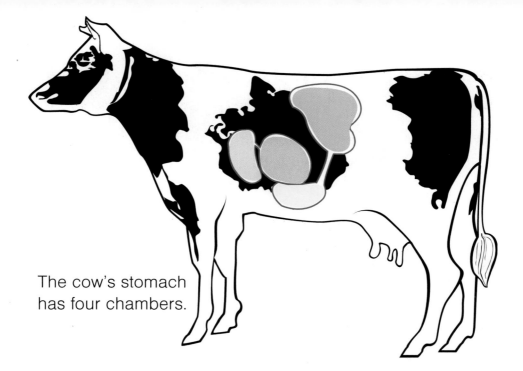

The cow's stomach
has four chambers.

A cow's stomach has four chambers. Each
chamber works to digest the cow's food. As the
cow eats, it chews very little. It swallows the food
into the first two stomach chambers. The food
waits there.

Have you seen a cow chew and chew? Farmers say the cow is "chewing her cud." The cow coughs up balls of food, or cud, from the first two stomachs. It chews the cud well. Then it swallows again. This time, the food goes into the third and fourth stomach chambers. They finish digesting the food.

The cow slowly chews her cud.

The cow's udder holds more than 1 gallon (4 l) of milk.

Some of the digested food enters the cow's bloodstream. Blood carries nutrients to the udder, where milk is made. To produce 1 gallon (4 l) of milk, 500 gallons (1,893 l) of blood must pass through the udder. Twice a day, a cow's udder fills with milk. Cows must be milked in the morning and evening.

A cow can begin producing milk when it has given birth to a calf. If the cow isn't milked regularly, its udder swells and hurts. Farmers who own small herds of cows might milk them by hand.

A farmer milks by hand.

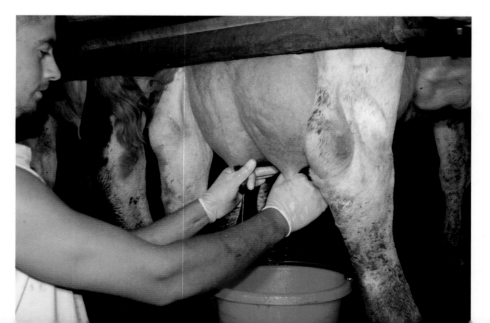

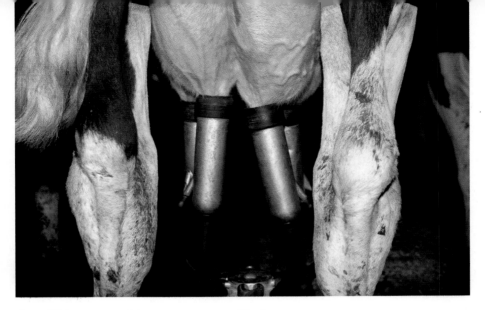

A milking machine pumps milk from
a cow's udder.

Today, most farmers use milking machines. They
pump the cow's milk from the udder. Milk straight
from the cow is warm.

Raw milk must be refrigerated quickly. Milk can spoil if it is not cooled right away. Refrigerated tank trucks collect the milk from farms. They take it to a dairy processing plant.

A tank truck carries milk from the dairy farm to the dairy plant.

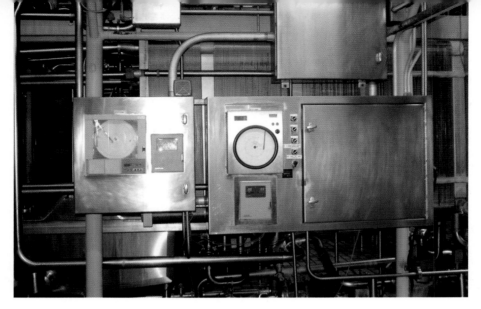

A pasteurizing machine heats raw milk.

In a Dairy Plant

In the dairy plant, milk is pasteurized. The milk is heated, and then it is cooled. Pasteurizing keeps milk from spoiling quickly. It also kills bacteria that could cause disease.

Another machine spins the whole milk. Spinning separates the cream. If all the cream is removed, nonfat or skim milk is left. The cream removed contains white fat. Low-fat and nonfat milk are not as white as whole milk.

A spinning machine separates cream from milk.

Stores sell different kinds of milk.

A bit of cream is left in some of the milk. This milk becomes 1% or 2% milk. The cream left in is 1% or 2% of the milk's weight. Another machine homogenizes the milk. It forces the milk through tiny holes. The white cream fat is broken down into tiny particles. The cream in the milk does not separate.

Every day, the dairy plants are cleaned. Workers sterilize all the machines. They wash all the equipment. Cleaning keeps mold and bacteria from forming in the machinery and the plant.

Workers spend a lot of time cleaning the plant and equipment.

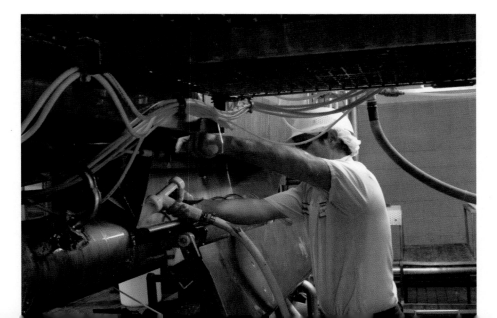

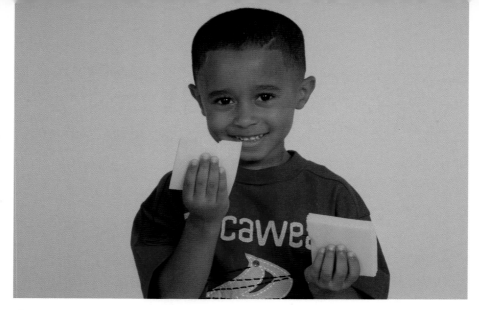

Several glasses of milk make one slice of cheese.

Yummy Foods from Milk

Many favorite foods begin as milk. Thank the dairy cow for cheese, yogurt, chocolate milk, ice cream, and cottage cheese. To make 1 gallon (4 l) of ice cream, it takes 12 pounds (5.4 kg) of milk. To make 1 pound (.5 kg) of cheese, it takes 10 pounds (4.5 kg) of milk. These milk products provide calcium and vitamins. They taste great, too!

Milk products can be combined with other ingredients. Dairy plants also make cream cheese, whipped cream, butter, and buttermilk. Dairy plants turn milk into many foods that help make strong bones and teeth.

How many milk products can you find on the shelves of your store?

Glossary

bacteria — tiny living organisms that can cause disease

calcium — a white substance that is found in milk, bones, and shells

digesting — breaking down food into a form that can be used by the body

hay — dried grass, clover, and other plants used to feed animals

mold — a fungus that forms a fuzzy coating on damp things

nutrients — substances that nourish or feed the body

protein — a substance found in all living plants and animals that is necessary to life

silos — tall, round buildings used to store food for animals

sterilize — to make free from germs

chamber — an enclosed space

udder — the baglike part of a cow that produces milk

For More Information

Books

Aliki. *Milk: From Cow to Carton*. NY: HarperCollins, 1992.

Gibbons, Gail. *The Milk Makers*. NY: Macmillan, 1985.

Llewellyn, Claire. *Milk. What's For Lunch?* Series. NY: Children's Press, 1998.

Taus-Bolstad, Stacy. *From Grass to Milk. Start to Finish* Series. Minneapolis: Lerner, 2003.

Web Sites

Holstein Heaven

www.nctc.net/counties/cow2/holstein.htm
Terrific cow photographs and videos

Moomilk Virtual Tour

www.moomilk.com/tours/tour1-1.htm
Great photos of cows and information about cows producing milk

Nutrition Information—The Milk Maze

www.nutritionexplorations.org/kids/activities/milkmaze.asp
Print and play the milk maze

Index

About the Author

Gretchen Will Mayo likes to be creative with her favorite foods. In her kitchen, broccoli and corn are mixed with oranges to make a salad. She sprinkles granola on applesauce. She blends yogurt with orange juice and bananas. She experiments with different pasta sauces. When she isn't eating, Ms. Mayo writes stories and books for young people like you. She is also a teacher and illustrator. She lives in Wisconsin with her husband, Tom, who makes delicious soups. They have three adult daughters.